To

_____

From

_____

Date

_____

The Lord your God is with you, He is mighty to save.
He will take great delight in you, He will quiet you
with His love, He will rejoice over you with singing.

Zephaniah 3:17

Whatever you do, work at it with all your heart,
as working for the Lord, not for men.
Colossians 3:23

The Lord is gracious and compassionate, slow to anger and rich in love. The Lord is good to all; He has compassion on all He has made.

Psalm 145:8-9

_____

_____

_____

_____

_____

_____

_____

_____

_____

_____

_____

_____

_____

_____

_____

_____

_____

_____

_____

_____

_____

_____

_____

"He will command His angels concerning you to guard you
carefully; they will lift you up in their hands, so
that you will not strike your foot against a stone."

Luke 4:10-11

The wisdom that comes from heaven is first of all pure; then peace-loving, considerate, submissive, full of mercy and good fruit, impartial and sincere. Peacemakers who sow in peace raise a harvest of righteousness.

James 3:17-18

_____

_____

_____

_____

_____

_____

_____

_____

_____

_____

_____

_____

_____

_____

_____

_____

_____

_____

_____

_____

_____

_____

_____

_____

You have been a refuge for the poor, a refuge for the needy in
his distress, a shelter from the storm and a shade from the heat.

Isaiah 25:4

This is what the Lord says: "Stand at the crossroads and look;
ask for the ancient paths, ask where the good way is,
and walk in it, and you will find rest for your souls."
Jeremiah 6:16

_____

The Lord replied, "My Presence will go with you, and I will give you rest."
Exodus 33:14

God demonstrates His own love for us in this:
While we were still sinners, Christ died for us.
Romans 5:8

Know therefore that the LORD your God is God; He is
the faithful God, keeping His covenant of love to a thousand
generations of those who love Him and keep His commands.

Deuteronomy 7:9

"Be strong and courageous. Do not be terrified; do not be discouraged,
for the LORD your God will be with you wherever you go."
Joshua 1:9

You have made known to me the path of life; You will fill me with
joy in Your presence, with eternal pleasures at Your right hand.
Psalm 16:11

_____

_____
_____
_____
_____
_____
_____
_____
_____
_____
_____
_____
_____
_____
_____
_____
_____
_____
_____
_____
_____
_____
_____

You alone are the LORD. You made the heavens, even the highest heavens, and all their starry host, the earth and all that is on it, the seas and all that is in them. You give life to everything, and the multitudes of heaven worship You.

Nehemiah 9:6

Whatever you do, whether in word or deed, do it all in the name
of the Lord Jesus, giving thanks to God the Father through Him.

Colossians 3:17

His divine power has given us everything we need for life and godliness
through our knowledge of Him who called us by His own glory and goodness.

2 Peter 1:3

If the LORD delights in a man's way, He makes his steps firm.
Psalm 37:23

Let us then approach the throne of grace with confidence, so that
we may receive mercy and find grace to help us in our time of need.

Hebrews 4:16

If we confess our sins, He is faithful and just and will forgive
us our sins and purify us from all unrighteousness.

1 John 1:9

So then, just as you received Christ Jesus as Lord, continue
to live in Him, rooted and built up in Him, strengthened in the
faith as you were taught, and overflowing with thankfulness.
Colossians 2:6-7

_____

The righteous cry out, and the LORD hears them; He delivers
them from all their troubles. The LORD is close to the
brokenhearted and saves those who are crushed in spirit.

Psalm 34:17-18

God is faithful; He will not let you be tempted beyond what
you can bear. But when you are tempted, He will
also provide a way out so that you can stand up under it.

1 Corinthians 10:13

_____

We know and rely on the love God has for us. God is love.
Whoever lives in love lives in God, and God in him.

1 John 4:16

Blessed are those who hunger and thirst for righteousness, for they will be filled. Blessed are the merciful, for they will be shown mercy.

Matthew 5:6-7

Let love and faithfulness never leave you; bind them
around your neck, write them on the tablet of your heart.

Proverbs 3:3

No eye has seen, no ear has heard, no mind has
conceived what God has prepared for those who love Him.
1 Corinthians 2:9

"I, the LORD, have called you in righteousness; I will take hold of your hand.
I will keep you and will make you to be a covenant for the people."

Isaiah 42:6

The prayer of a righteous man is powerful and effective.

James 5:16

_____

"I tell you the truth, if you have faith as small as a mustard seed,
you can say to this mountain, 'Move from here to there'
and it will move. Nothing will be impossible for you."
Matthew 17:20

I will give You thanks, for You answered me;
You have become my salvation.
Psalm 118:21

To the man who pleases Him,
God gives wisdom, knowledge and happiness.
Ecclesiastes 2:26

Blessed is the man who perseveres under trial, because
when he has stood the test, he will receive the crown
of life that God has promised to those who love Him.

James 1:12

_____

"Fear not, for I have redeemed you;
I have summoned you by name; you are Mine."
Isaiah 43:1

The Lord your God is with you, He is mighty to save.
He will take great delight in you, He will quiet you
with His love, He will rejoice over you with singing.
Zephaniah 3:17

Whatever you do, work at it with all your heart,
as working for the Lord, not for men.
Colossians 3:23

The Lord is gracious and compassionate, slow to anger and rich in love. The Lord is good to all; He has compassion on all He has made.

Psalm 145:8-9

_____

"He will command His angels concerning you to guard you
carefully; they will lift you up in their hands, so
that you will not strike your foot against a stone."

Luke 4:10-11

The wisdom that comes from heaven is first of all pure; then peace-loving, considerate, submissive, full of mercy and good fruit, impartial and sincere. Peacemakers who sow in peace raise a harvest of righteousness.

James 3:17-18

_____

You have been a refuge for the poor, a refuge for the needy in
his distress, a shelter from the storm and a shade from the heat.
Isaiah 25:4

This is what the LORD says: "Stand at the crossroads and look;
ask for the ancient paths, ask where the good way is,
and walk in it, and you will find rest for your souls."

Jeremiah 6:16

The Lord replied, "My Presence will go with you, and I will give you rest."
Exodus 33:14

God demonstrates His own love for us in this:
While we were still sinners, Christ died for us.
Romans 5:8

_____

Know therefore that the LORD your God is God; He is
the faithful God, keeping His covenant of love to a thousand
generations of those who love Him and keep His commands.

Deuteronomy 7:9

_____

_____
_____
_____
_____
_____
_____
_____
_____
_____
_____
_____
_____
_____
_____
_____
_____
_____
_____
_____
_____
_____
_____
_____

"Be strong and courageous. Do not be terrified; do not be discouraged,
for the LORD your God will be with you wherever you go."

Joshua 1:9

You have made known to me the path of life; You will fill me with
joy in Your presence, with eternal pleasures at Your right hand.

Psalm 16:11

You alone are the LORD. You made the heavens, even the highest heavens, and all their starry host, the earth and all that is on it, the seas and all that is in them. You give life to everything, and the multitudes of heaven worship You.

Nehemiah 9:6

Whatever you do, whether in word or deed, do it all in the name
of the Lord Jesus, giving thanks to God the Father through Him.

Colossians 3:17

His divine power has given us everything we need for life and godliness
through our knowledge of Him who called us by His own glory and goodness.

2 Peter 1:3

_____

If the LORD delights in a man's way, He makes his steps firm.
Psalm 37:23

Let us then approach the throne of grace with confidence, so that
we may receive mercy and find grace to help us in our time of need.

Hebrews 4:16

_____

If we confess our sins, He is faithful and just and will forgive
us our sins and purify us from all unrighteousness.
1 John 1:9

So then, just as you received Christ Jesus as Lord, continue
to live in Him, rooted and built up in Him, strengthened in the
faith as you were taught, and overflowing with thankfulness.
Colossians 2:6-7

_____

The righteous cry out, and the Lord hears them; He delivers
them from all their troubles. The Lord is close to the
brokenhearted and saves those who are crushed in spirit.

Psalm 34:17-18

God is faithful; He will not let you be tempted beyond what
you can bear. But when you are tempted, He will
also provide a way out so that you can stand up under it.
1 Corinthians 10:13

We know and rely on the love God has for us. God is love.
Whoever lives in love lives in God, and God in him.

1 John 4:16

Blessed are those who hunger and thirst for righteousness, for they
will be filled. Blessed are the merciful, for they will be shown mercy.

Matthew 5:6-7

_____

Let love and faithfulness never leave you; bind them
around your neck, write them on the tablet of your heart.

Proverbs 3:3

No eye has seen, no ear has heard, no mind has
conceived what God has prepared for those who love Him.
1 Corinthians 2:9

_____

_____

_____

_____

_____

_____

_____

_____

_____

_____

_____

_____

_____

_____

_____

_____

_____

_____

_____

_____

_____

_____

_____

"I, the LORD, have called you in righteousness; I will take hold of your hand.
I will keep you and will make you to be a covenant for the people."

Isaiah 42:6

The prayer of a righteous man is powerful and effective.

James 5:16

_____

"I tell you the truth, if you have faith as small as a mustard seed,
you can say to this mountain, 'Move from here to there'
and it will move. Nothing will be impossible for you."
Matthew 17:20

I will give You thanks, for You answered me;
You have become my salvation.
Psalm 118:21

_____

To the man who pleases Him,
God gives wisdom, knowledge and happiness.
Ecclesiastes 2:26

Blessed is the man who perseveres under trial, because
when he has stood the test, he will receive the crown
of life that God has promised to those who love Him.

James 1:12

"Fear not, for I have redeemed you;
I have summoned you by name; you are Mine."
Isaiah 43:1

The LORD your God is with you, He is mighty to save.
He will take great delight in you, He will quiet you
with His love, He will rejoice over you with singing.

Zephaniah 3:17

Whatever you do, work at it with all your heart,
as working for the Lord, not for men.
Colossians 3:23

The LORD is gracious and compassionate, slow to anger and rich in love. The LORD is good to all; He has compassion on all He has made.

Psalm 145:8-9

_____

"He will command His angels concerning you to guard you
carefully; they will lift you up in their hands, so
that you will not strike your foot against a stone."

Luke 4:10-11

The wisdom that comes from heaven is first of all pure; then peace-loving, considerate, submissive, full of mercy and good fruit, impartial and sincere. Peacemakers who sow in peace raise a harvest of righteousness.

James 3:17-18

_____

You have been a refuge for the poor, a refuge for the needy in
his distress, a shelter from the storm and a shade from the heat.
Isaiah 25:4

This is what the LORD says: "Stand at the crossroads and look;
ask for the ancient paths, ask where the good way is,
and walk in it, and you will find rest for your souls."
Jeremiah 6:16

The LORD replied, "My Presence will go with you, and I will give you rest."
Exodus 33:14

God demonstrates His own love for us in this:
While we were still sinners, Christ died for us.

Romans 5:8

Know therefore that the LORD your God is God; He is
the faithful God, keeping His covenant of love to a thousand
generations of those who love Him and keep His commands.

Deuteronomy 7:9

"Be strong and courageous. Do not be terrified; do not be discouraged,
for the LORD your God will be with you wherever you go."

Joshua 1:9

_____

You have made known to me the path of life; You will fill me with
joy in Your presence, with eternal pleasures at Your right hand.
Psalm 16:11

You alone are the LORD. You made the heavens, even the highest heavens, and all their starry host, the earth and all that is on it, the seas and all that is in them. You give life to everything, and the multitudes of heaven worship You.

Nehemiah 9:6

Whatever you do, whether in word or deed, do it all in the name
of the Lord Jesus, giving thanks to God the Father through Him.

Colossians 3:17

His divine power has given us everything we need for life and godliness
through our knowledge of Him who called us by His own glory and goodness.

2 Peter 1:3

If the LORD delights in a man's way, He makes his steps firm.
Psalm 37:23

Let us then approach the throne of grace with confidence, so that
we may receive mercy and find grace to help us in our time of need.
Hebrews 4:16

_____

If we confess our sins, He is faithful and just and will forgive
us our sins and purify us from all unrighteousness.
1 John 1:9

So then, just as you received Christ Jesus as Lord, continue
to live in Him, rooted and built up in Him, strengthened in the
faith as you were taught, and overflowing with thankfulness.

Colossians 2:6-7

The righteous cry out, and the LORD hears them; He delivers them from all their troubles. The LORD is close to the brokenhearted and saves those who are crushed in spirit.

Psalm 34:17-18

God is faithful; He will not let you be tempted beyond what
you can bear. But when you are tempted, He will
also provide a way out so that you can stand up under it.
1 Corinthians 10:13

We know and rely on the love God has for us. God is love.
Whoever lives in love lives in God, and God in him.

1 John 4:16

Blessed are those who hunger and thirst for righteousness, for they
will be filled. Blessed are the merciful, for they will be shown mercy.
Matthew 5:6-7

Let love and faithfulness never leave you; bind them
around your neck, write them on the tablet of your heart.

Proverbs 3:3

No eye has seen, no ear has heard, no mind has
conceived what God has prepared for those who love Him.

1 Corinthians 2:9

_____

"I, the LORD, have called you in righteousness; I will take hold of your hand.
I will keep you and will make you to be a covenant for the people."

Isaiah 42:6

The prayer of a righteous man is powerful and effective.

James 5:16

"I tell you the truth, if you have faith as small as a mustard seed,
you can say to this mountain, 'Move from here to there'
and it will move. Nothing will be impossible for you."
Matthew 17:20

I will give You thanks, for You answered me;
You have become my salvation.
Psalm 118:21

_____

To the man who pleases Him,
God gives wisdom, knowledge and happiness.
Ecclesiastes 2:26

Blessed is the man who perseveres under trial, because
when he has stood the test, he will receive the crown
of life that God has promised to those who love Him.

James 1:12

_____

"Fear not, for I have redeemed you;
I have summoned you by name; you are Mine."
Isaiah 43:1

The LORD your God is with you, He is mighty to save.
He will take great delight in you, He will quiet you
with His love, He will rejoice over you with singing.
Zephaniah 3:17

Whatever you do, work at it with all your heart,
as working for the Lord, not for men.
Colossians 3:23

The LORD is gracious and compassionate, slow to anger and rich in love. The LORD is good to all; He has compassion on all He has made.

Psalm 145:8-9

_____

"He will command His angels concerning you to guard you
carefully; they will lift you up in their hands, so
that you will not strike your foot against a stone."

Luke 4:10-11

The wisdom that comes from heaven is first of all pure; then peace-loving, considerate, submissive, full of mercy and good fruit, impartial and sincere. Peacemakers who sow in peace raise a harvest of righteousness.

James 3:17-18

_____

You have been a refuge for the poor, a refuge for the needy in
his distress, a shelter from the storm and a shade from the heat.
Isaiah 25:4

This is what the LORD says: "Stand at the crossroads and look;
ask for the ancient paths, ask where the good way is,
and walk in it, and you will find rest for your souls."
Jeremiah 6:16

The LORD replied, "My Presence will go with you, and I will give you rest."
Exodus 33:14

God demonstrates His own love for us in this:
While we were still sinners, Christ died for us.

Romans 5:8

Know therefore that the LORD your God is God; He is
the faithful God, keeping His covenant of love to a thousand
generations of those who love Him and keep His commands.

Deuteronomy 7:9

"Be strong and courageous. Do not be terrified; do not be discouraged, for the Lord your God will be with you wherever you go."

Joshua 1:9

You have made known to me the path of life; You will fill me with
joy in Your presence, with eternal pleasures at Your right hand.
Psalm 16:11

You alone are the LORD. You made the heavens, even the highest heavens, and all their starry host, the earth and all that is on it, the seas and all that is in them. You give life to everything, and the multitudes of heaven worship You.

Nehemiah 9:6

Whatever you do, whether in word or deed, do it all in the name
of the Lord Jesus, giving thanks to God the Father through Him.

Colossians 3:17

His divine power has given us everything we need for life and godliness
through our knowledge of Him who called us by His own glory and goodness.

2 Peter 1:3

_____

If the LORD delights in a man's way, He makes his steps firm.
Psalm 37:23

Let us then approach the throne of grace with confidence, so that
we may receive mercy and find grace to help us in our time of need.

Hebrews 4:16

If we confess our sins, He is faithful and just and will forgive
us our sins and purify us from all unrighteousness.
1 John 1:9

So then, just as you received Christ Jesus as Lord, continue
to live in Him, rooted and built up in Him, strengthened in the
faith as you were taught, and overflowing with thankfulness.

Colossians 2:6-7

The righteous cry out, and the LORD hears them; He delivers
them from all their troubles. The LORD is close to the
brokenhearted and saves those who are crushed in spirit.
Psalm 34:17-18

God is faithful; He will not let you be tempted beyond what
you can bear. But when you are tempted, He will
also provide a way out so that you can stand up under it.
1 Corinthians 10:13

We know and rely on the love God has for us. God is love.
Whoever lives in love lives in God, and God in him.

1 John 4:16

Blessed are those who hunger and thirst for righteousness, for they will be filled. Blessed are the merciful, for they will be shown mercy.

Matthew 5:6-7

Let love and faithfulness never leave you; bind them
around your neck, write them on the tablet of your heart.

Proverbs 3:3

No eye has seen, no ear has heard, no mind has
conceived what God has prepared for those who love Him.
1 Corinthians 2:9

"I, the LORD, have called you in righteousness; I will take hold of your hand. I will keep you and will make you to be a covenant for the people."

Isaiah 42:6

The prayer of a righteous man is powerful and effective.

James 5:16

"I tell you the truth, if you have faith as small as a mustard seed,
you can say to this mountain, 'Move from here to there'
and it will move. Nothing will be impossible for you."
Matthew 17:20

I will give You thanks, for You answered me;
You have become my salvation.
Psalm 118:21

_____

To the man who pleases Him,
God gives wisdom, knowledge and happiness.
Ecclesiastes 2:26

Blessed is the man who perseveres under trial, because
when he has stood the test, he will receive the crown
of life that God has promised to those who love Him.

James 1:12

_____

"Fear not, for I have redeemed you;
I have summoned you by name; you are Mine."
Isaiah 43:1

The Lord your God is with you, He is mighty to save.
He will take great delight in you, He will quiet you
with His love, He will rejoice over you with singing.
Zephaniah 3:17

Whatever you do, work at it with all your heart,
as working for the Lord, not for men.
Colossians 3:23

The LORD is gracious and compassionate, slow to anger and rich in love. The LORD is good to all; He has compassion on all He has made.

Psalm 145:8-9

_____

"He will command His angels concerning you to guard you
carefully; they will lift you up in their hands, so
that you will not strike your foot against a stone."

Luke 4:10-11

The wisdom that comes from heaven is first of all pure; then peace-loving,
considerate, submissive, full of mercy and good fruit, impartial and sincere.
Peacemakers who sow in peace raise a harvest of righteousness.

James 3:17-18

_____

_____

_____

_____

_____

_____

_____

_____

_____

_____

_____

_____

_____

_____

_____

_____

_____

_____

_____

_____

_____

_____

You have been a refuge for the poor, a refuge for the needy in
his distress, a shelter from the storm and a shade from the heat.

Isaiah 25:4

This is what the LORD says: "Stand at the crossroads and look;
ask for the ancient paths, ask where the good way is,
and walk in it, and you will find rest for your souls."
Jeremiah 6:16

The Lord replied, "My Presence will go with you, and I will give you rest."
Exodus 33:14

God demonstrates His own love for us in this:
While we were still sinners, Christ died for us.

Romans 5:8

Know therefore that the LORD your God is God; He is
the faithful God, keeping His covenant of love to a thousand
generations of those who love Him and keep His commands.

Deuteronomy 7:9

"Be strong and courageous. Do not be terrified; do not be discouraged,
for the Lord your God will be with you wherever you go."

Joshua 1:9

_____

You have made known to me the path of life; You will fill me with
joy in Your presence, with eternal pleasures at Your right hand.

Psalm 16:11

You alone are the LORD. You made the heavens, even the highest heavens, and all their starry host, the earth and all that is on it, the seas and all that is in them. You give life to everything, and the multitudes of heaven worship You.

Nehemiah 9:6

Whatever you do, whether in word or deed, do it all in the name
of the Lord Jesus, giving thanks to God the Father through Him.

Colossians 3:17

His divine power has given us everything we need for life and godliness
through our knowledge of Him who called us by His own glory and goodness.
2 Peter 1:3

_____

If the LORD delights in a man's way, He makes his steps firm.
Psalm 37:23

Let us then approach the throne of grace with confidence, so that
we may receive mercy and find grace to help us in our time of need.

Hebrews 4:16

If we confess our sins, He is faithful and just and will forgive
us our sins and purify us from all unrighteousness.

1 John 1:9

So then, just as you received Christ Jesus as Lord, continue
to live in Him, rooted and built up in Him, strengthened in the
faith as you were taught, and overflowing with thankfulness.

Colossians 2:6-7

The righteous cry out, and the LORD hears them; He delivers
them from all their troubles. The LORD is close to the
brokenhearted and saves those who are crushed in spirit.
Psalm 34:17-18

God is faithful; He will not let you be tempted beyond what
you can bear. But when you are tempted, He will
also provide a way out so that you can stand up under it.

1 Corinthians 10:13

We know and rely on the love God has for us. God is love.
Whoever lives in love lives in God, and God in him.

1 John 4:16

Blessed are those who hunger and thirst for righteousness, for they
will be filled. Blessed are the merciful, for they will be shown mercy.

Matthew 5:6-7

Let love and faithfulness never leave you; bind them
around your neck, write them on the tablet of your heart.

Proverbs 3:3

No eye has seen, no ear has heard, no mind has
conceived what God has prepared for those who love Him.
1 Corinthians 2:9

_____

"I, the LORD, have called you in righteousness; I will take hold of your hand.
I will keep you and will make you to be a covenant for the people."
Isaiah 42:6

The prayer of a righteous man is powerful and effective.

James 5:16

_____

"I tell you the truth, if you have faith as small as a mustard seed,
you can say to this mountain, 'Move from here to there'
and it will move. Nothing will be impossible for you."
Matthew 17:20

I will give You thanks, for You answered me;
You have become my salvation.
Psalm 118:21

_____

To the man who pleases Him,
God gives wisdom, knowledge and happiness.
Ecclesiastes 2:26